Longman Structural Rea[der]
Stage 3

Seven One Act Plays

Donn Byrne

Illustrated by Barry Wilkinson

Vivian Lau

LONGMAN

LONGMAN GROUP UK LIMITED
Longman House, Burnt Mill
Harlow, Essex CM20 2JE, England
and Associated Companies throughout the world.

© Longman Group Ltd 1970

All rights reserved; no part of this publication may be
reproduced, stored in a retrieval system, or transmitted
in any form or by any means, electronic, mechanical,
photocopying, recording, or otherwise, without
the prior written permission of the Publishers.

*First published *1970*
*New impressions *1970; *1971;*
*1972; *1973; * 1974; *1977(twice);*
*1979; *1980; *1982; *1983; *1985(twice); *1986(twice);*
*1988; *1989; *1990; *1991; *1992; *1993.*

ISBN 0-582-53737-1

Produced by Longman Singapore Publishers Pte Ltd
Printed in Singapore

Longman Structural Readers

It is today widely held that it is the structure of a language, rather than the vocabulary, which causes the greatest difficulty to the foreign learner. The supplementary readers in this series are therefore based on the principles of structure control.

Up-to-date English courses have, at each stage, a certain common content of sentence-patterns. This common content, which will be familiar to the learner at the end of each stage, is represented in the structure tables developed to govern the preparation of the series (see *A Handbook to Longman Structural Readers* for the structure tables and basic vocabulary).

Control of vocabulary is also maintained (as in many existing series of supplementary readers) and one new principle has been introduced. Content words outside the given basic vocabulary but of value in the story are introduced freely within the structural limits by a prescribed process of repetition.

The learner's pleasure in reading is thus increased, and with the strict control of useful structures, the development of a sense of achievement will be aided and the maximum value derived from the practice of supplementary reading.

Other titles at Stage 3 of Longman Structural Readers

1 Recommended for use with children (aged 8–12)
2 Recommended for use with young people (aged 12–15)
3 Recommended for use with older people (aged 15 plus)
No figure: recommended for use with all ages

General Fiction

Biggles Breaks the Silence
  Captain W E John **(2)**
The Brumby
  M E Patchett
Clint Magee
  L G Alexander
Dangerous Game
  William Harris/L G Alexander
David and Marianne
  John Dent **(2.3)**
David Copperfield
  Charles Dickens
Down the River
  Donn Byrne **(1.2)**
Good Morning, Mexico!
  L G Alexander **(3)**
The Last Experiment
  Lewis Jones
Mark and Jennifer
  John Dent
Mosquito Town
  N Adoma and A G Eyre
The Munich Connection
  Peter Cooper
Operation Mastermind
  L G Alexander
Round the World in Eighty Days
  Jules Verne
Smith
  Leon Garfield
Treasure Island
  R L Stevenson **(1.2)**
Ulster Story
  Michel Villeneuve

Short Stories

Catch a Thief
Looking at Life
Love is a Gimmick and Other
  Short Stories
  Paul Gallico
Nothing But the Best and Other
  Short Stories
Short Stories from Dr Finlay's
  Casebook
  A J Cronin
The Spy and Other Stories,
  Paul Victor
Stories of Today
True or Not?

Adventure

Everest the Hard Way
  Chris Bonington and Neville Grant
SOS in Space
  Lewis Jones **(2.3)**
Stunt!
  Lewis Jones
Survive the Savage Sea
  *Dougal Robertson and Roy
  Kingsbury*

Background

Great British Ghosts
  Nick McIver

Non Fiction

How Life Began
  Lewis Jones
Tales from Arab History
The World Under the Sea
  A Wright and M Buckby

Famous People

Gandhi
  Donn Byrne
Some Unusual People

Plays

Inspector Thackeray Calls
  Kenneth James and Lloyd Mullen
  (2.3)
Seven One-Act Plays
  Donn Byrne

Contents

Please, Mr Smith...!

LET THE BOY SPEAK

Characters

MR SMITH, a greengrocer
MISS WHITE
MRS BALL }customers in the shop
MRS WOOD
JOHNNY BELL, a small boy

A greengrocer's shop. Mr Smith is serving behind the counter. One customer is going out. Three women are waiting in the shop.

MR SMITH: Yes? Who's next, please?

MISS WHITE: I think you're next, Mrs Ball. You were here before me, weren't you?

MRS BALL: Oh, was I?

MR SMITH: What can I do for you, madam? Do you need any fruit?

MRS BALL: Let me see. Ah, yes! I want . . .

A small boy runs into the greengrocer's shop. He pushes his way between the women and stands in front of the counter.

JOHNNY: Please, Mr Smith . . . !

MR SMITH (*not letting him continue*): One moment, young fellow! I'm serving this lady. And *these* two ladies are waiting. (*He turns to Mrs Ball again.*) Yes, madam. What were you saying?

JOHNNY: But, sir!

MRS BALL: Be quiet! I want three pounds of potatoes, Mr Smith.

MR SMITH: Three pounds of potatoes. Certainly. I have some good ones here. (*He points to the potatoes near the counter.*) Three pence a pound. Are these all right?

MRS BALL: Yes, I'll take those.

MRS WOOD (*looking at Johnny*): The children today! They push in!

MISS WHITE: They can't wait! They want to be first!

MRS WOOD: How old are you?

JOHNNY: Nine, madam.

MRS WOOD: Only nine! And you pushed in front of this lady.

JOHNNY: I had to. I wanted . . .

MISS WHITE (*not letting him finish*): Young people must learn to wait. You can't push in front of people. You're not the *only* customer in the shop, are you?

JOHNNY: No, madam.

MRS BALL: Did your mother send you?

JOHNNY: No. I wanted . . .

MRS WOOD (*quickly*): Ah, you wanted something for yourself! You couldn't wait, could you? What's your name?

JOHNNY: Johnny Bell.

MISS WHITE: You live in Church Street, don't you? I've seen you there.

JOHNNY: Yes, madam.

MISS WHITE: Yes, I know your mother. I'll speak to her about you.

JOHNNY: But I only wanted . . .

MR SMITH: That's enough, young man. We don't want to hear. (*He turns to Mrs Ball.*) Here you are, Mrs Ball. Three pounds of potatoes. Is that all? That'll be nine pence, please. Thank you.

Mrs Ball gives Mr Smith nine pence. She takes her potatoes and leaves.

MR SMITH: Next, please.

JOHNNY: I'm sorry but . . . (*No one listens to Johnny.*)

MISS WHITE: I want some apples, please. Two pounds.

MR SMITH: What about these? (*He points to some apples on the counter.*) They're only fifteen pence a pound.

MISS WHITE: No, they look rather green. Have you any sweet ones?

MR SMITH: Certainly, madam. I have some good ones but they're still in my car. Twenty pence a pound.

MISS WHITE: Can I see them?

MR SMITH: I'll go and get them.

Mr Smith goes out of the shop. After a minute he runs in again.

MR SMITH (*shouting*): They're not there! There was a box of

They're not there!

apples in my car and now it's gone. The car's empty.

JOHNNY: I saw two men near your car, Mr Smith. They opened the door and took out a box of apples.

MR SMITH: My apples! I've lost a big box of apples. (*He turns to Johnny and shouts in an angry voice.*) Why didn't you tell me?

JOHNNY: I wanted to tell you, sir, but no one let me speak!

THE END

Well, the room's ready

THE RIGHT PERSON

Characters

MARY STONE
HARRY STONE, her husband
YOUNG MAN
OLD MAN

A room in the Stones' house. It is on the first floor. Mrs Stone wants to let the room. She is standing beside her husband.

MRS STONE: Well, the room's ready. I've worked very hard. I hope I can let it. What do you think?

MR STONE: Oh, it's all right. You'll be able to let it. People need rooms.

MRS STONE: But *you* don't like it very much. I can see that. But what's wrong with it? Tell me. It's big enough, isn't it?

MR STONE: Yes, it's certainly not a small room.

MRS STONE: And it's clean, too.

MR STONE: Yes, it's clean.

MRS STONE: What's wrong, then? Is it the furniture? Perhaps you don't like that.

MR STONE: Well, it *is* rather heavy. And old, too.

MRS STONE: But it's very good furniture. It belonged to my mother.

MR STONE: That's the trouble. It may be good, but it's rather old. People like different furniture today. They don't like heavy things in their rooms.

MRS STONE: That's not true. People go to the shops and buy old furniture like this.

MR STONE: Yes, but those people won't come here. They have their *own* houses. But why do you want to let a room? It isn't necessary. We've got enough money, haven't we? People only let rooms if they haven't enough money.

MRS STONE: Yes, of course we have enough money. That isn't the reason.

5

MR STONE: What is the reason, then?

MRS STONE: I want something to do. I'm in the house all day. You won't let me work in your office.

MR STONE: No, you can't do that. But you can work in the garden. I'll let you do that!

MRS STONE: No, thank you. I don't want to work in the garden.

MR STONE: Well, I hope a nice person takes the room. A quiet person. I don't want a lot of noise in the house.

MRS STONE: I'll let it to the right person. A nice young man. Two people are coming this morning. They telephoned last night. They'll be here soon.

MR STONE: You haven't wasted any time!

What have I done now?

Mrs Stone crosses to the window. Her husband follows. They both look out of the window.

MRS STONE: The room has a nice view, hasn't it? You can see for miles.

MR STONE: Yes, it's a nice view. But people won't take the room only for the view. (*He points out of the window.*) Look, a young man's coming to the house.

MRS STONE (*looking at her watch*): Yes, that's the first. He's on time. I liked his voice when he telephoned. He spoke very nicely. I think he comes from a good family.

MR STONE: Well, he won't like *this* room!

The doorbell rings.

MR STONE (*after a moment*): Well, dear. Aren't you going to open the door? The young man's waiting. Shall I go?

The doorbell rings again.

MRS STONE: No, *I'll* go. *You* stay here and wait. I'll bring him up.

Mrs Stone goes out. Mr Stone walks round the room and then stops in front of the fireplace.

MR STONE (*talking to himself*): Hm, this wall doesn't look very strong.

He pushes the wall rather hard and a piece falls out.

MR STONE: Oh dear! What have I done now? I hope the young man doesn't see the hole.

At that moment Mrs Stone returns. The young man follows her into the room.

MRS STONE: Well, this is the room. I hope you like it.

YOUNG MAN (*standing and looking round the room*): Hm.

MRS STONE: Do you like it?

YOUNG MAN: I was looking for a bigger room.

MRS STONE: This room is quite big. The rooms are smaller in some houses.

YOUNG MAN: And this furniture! It's rather old, isn't it? Where did you find it?

MRS STONE (*rather coldly*): It belonged to my mother. It's very good furniture. She always paid a lot of money for her furniture.

YOUNG MAN: I see. It belonged to your mother. Now I understand. (*He crosses the room and sits down on the bed.*)

This bed's rather hard

This bed's rather hard. I like a soft one. I can't sleep on a bed like this. It's like wood!

MRS STONE: Oh, we can change the bed. We'll get a soft one for you.

The young man gets up and walks to the window. He looks out.

MR STONE: It's a nice view, isn't it? Do you like it? You can see for miles.

YOUNG MAN: Can you? Views don't interest me. I'm out all day. You can't look at views when it's dark.

The young man walks across the room. He stops in front of the fireplace. He sees the hole in the wall.

YOUNG MAN: Look at this hole. The wall's falling down!

MRS STONE (*seeing the hole for the first time*): I've never seen that hole before. (*She turns to her husband.*) When did that happen?

MR STONE: A few minutes ago. You were out of the room.

MRS STONE: Did *you* do it?

MR STONE: I only touched it and a piece fell out. It's all right. I can repair it.

Mrs Stone gives her husband an angry look.

YOUNG MAN: It's an old house. These things happen, of course.

MRS STONE: My husband can soon repair it.

YOUNG MAN: I'm sure the room's cold in the winter. I'm not very strong.

MRS STONE: We'll put a good fire in the room. You won't be cold. I'll look after you like a mother!

YOUNG MAN: And how much do you want for the room?

MRS STONE: Five pounds a week.

YOUNG MAN: Five pounds! That's a lot of money for this room.

MRS STONE: With breakfast. I'll give you a good breakfast.

YOUNG MAN: But I don't eat breakfast. I get up late, so I don't have time. I only take a cup of tea.

MRS STONE: Then you can have the room for four pounds. And I'll wash your clothes for you.

YOUNG MAN: I must think about it. I can't give you an answer now.

MRS STONE: Yes, I understand. But a second person is coming this morning. He may want the room.

YOUNG MAN (*already going to the door*): I'll telephone you this afternoon. Is that all right?

MRS STONE: Yes, of course. But please don't forget.

YOUNG MAN: Thank you. Goodbye.

MRS STONE (*to her husband*): Can you go to the door with the young man, Harry?

Mr Stone goes out with the young man. After a short time he comes back.

MRS STONE: Do you think he wants the room?

MR STONE: No, of course not. He didn't like it. You could see that. He won't telephone.

MRS STONE: I hope he takes it. I liked him.

MR STONE: *I* didn't!

MRS STONE (*in an angry voice*): And that hole over the fireplace! Why did you do that?

MR STONE: I told you, dear. I only touched the wall and a piece fell out.

MRS STONE: It isn't possible.

At that moment the doorbell rings again. They cross to the window and look out.

MR STONE: There's an old man at the door.

MRS STONE: Is he the second person? I thought he was younger. He doesn't look very clean.

MR STONE: Shall I go and open the door?

MRS STONE: Can't we stay here? He doesn't know we're in. Perhaps he won't wait.

The doorbell rings again.

MR STONE: He knows we're in the house. Perhaps he saw the young man when he came out.

MRS STONE: But what shall I say to him? I don't want to look after an old man. He may get ill.

MR STONE: But you must let him see the room. Perhaps he has come a long way.

MRS STONE: All right. Let him come in. But he can't have the room.

Mr Stone goes out. He comes back with the old man.

OLD MAN: Good morning, Mrs Stone. My name's Arthur Dean. I telephoned you about the room.

MRS STONE: Yes, I know. But I'm very sorry. A person has already taken the room.

OLD MAN: Already?

MRS STONE: Yes, I've let it. A young man came a short time ago and he's taken the room.

OLD MAN: Oh, I met a young man near your house. Perhaps it was the same person. I stopped him in the street and asked him the way.

MR STONE: Yes, that was the young man. He left a few minutes ago.

OLD MAN: But he said he didn't want the room.

MR STONE: Oh, did he say that? (*He looks at his wife.*)

OLD MAN: Yes. He told me he didn't like the room. (*He looks round the room.*) But it's very nice. *I* like it.

My name's Arthur Dean

MRS STONE: We live a long way from the town. There aren't a lot of buses. Only one an hour.

OLD MAN: Oh, that doesn't matter. I don't go to work. When I go to town, I can walk. I enjoy a walk. And your house is very quiet. Few houses are quiet like this.

MRS STONE: It's quiet at the moment. But my husband makes a lot of noise. And I like to listen to the radio. The house isn't very quiet then.

OLD MAN: Oh, that's quite different. I was talking about the noise of cars and buses.

MRS STONE: The room's rather cold in winter.

OLD MAN: I won't notice it. I may be old, but I'm still very strong. (*He crosses to the window.*) It's a nice view from here. I like a room with a view.

MR STONE: Yes, it *is* nice, isn't it?

MRS STONE: It's nice now. But they're going to build houses over there. When that happens, there won't be a view.

OLD MAN: Perhaps they'll never build them. Who knows?

MR STONE: What about the furniture? Do you like that?

OLD MAN: Yes, very much. I like old furniture.

MRS STONE: I'm afraid the bed's very hard. Go and try it.

OLD MAN: It's not necessary. I like a hard bed. Yes, I like this room very much. I was looking for a room like this. I hope it doesn't cost a lot.

MRS STONE: Five pounds a week.

OLD MAN: Five pounds. Well, that's not much for this room. I was ready to pay six for a good room. Is that with breakfast?

MR STONE: Yes, with breakfast.

MRS STONE: Of course the room isn't quite ready. Look at that wall. (*She points to the wall over the fireplace.*) We'll have to repair it. It will take time.

OLD MAN: Oh, that doesn't matter. I can put a picture over the hole. That will cover it.

MR STONE: We have some old pictures. Where are they, Mary? They're still in the attic, aren't they?

MRS STONE: Yes, I put them in the attic. I didn't like them.

OLD MAN: Well, we can put one of those over the hole.

MR STONE: I'll go and get one or two. You can have a look at them. (*He goes out of the room.*)

MRS STONE: You said you didn't work, Mr Dean.

OLD MAN: That's right. I stopped work two years ago.

MRS STONE: Where did you work?

OLD MAN: In a museum.

MRS STONE: What did you do in the museum?

OLD MAN: I was in charge of the pictures, in fact. I know a lot about pictures. I'm writing a book about them. So I need a quiet room. Like a museum!

MRS STONE: Yes, I see.

Mr Stone comes back with the pictures. He has one big picture and two smaller ones.

MRS STONE: Mr Dean used to work in a museum, Harry. He knows a lot about pictures.

MR STONE: Well, he won't like these! They're very dirty.

Mr Dean looks at the pictures.

OLD MAN: Well, this big one will cover the hole.

MR STONE: Do you like it?

OLD MAN: It's not a bad picture. I'll clean it for you. I know about these things. (*He picks up one of the smaller pictures.*) Well, this *is* a surprise!

MR STONE: What is it?

The old man takes the picture to the window. He looks at it with great care.

Mr Stone comes back with the pictures

OLD MAN: Is this really yours?

MR STONE: Yes, of course. All these pictures belonged to my wife's mother. Why? Is it a good picture?

OLD MAN: Yes, it is. It's by John Holland. Look, you can see his name here. In the corner of the picture.

MRS STONE: Who was he? I've never heard of him. Did he paint good pictures?

OLD MAN: Yes, he painted some very good pictures. He lived about a hundred years ago. People didn't like his pictures then, but they like them now.

MR STONE: I see. And is the picture worth much?

OLD MAN: Oh, yes. It's worth quite a lot of money. It may be worth a thousand pounds.

MR STONE: A thousand pounds! Did you hear that, Mary? This little picture may be worth a thousand pounds! And we put it in the attic.

Look, you can see his name here

MRS STONE: I can't believe it.

MR STONE: And there are a lot of pictures in the attic.

OLD MAN: Well, I must look at all of them. (*To Mrs Stone*.) But perhaps you don't want to let the room now. You'll be rich when you sell the pictures.

MRS STONE: No, of course you must have the room. And I'll be able to buy new furniture with the money.

OLD MAN: No, please don't do that! Not for me. I like this old furniture. Don't change it. I'm sure I'll be very happy here.

THE END

We've found a nice place

AN AFTERNOON ON THE BEACH

Characters

MR BROWN
MRS BROWN
JOHN ⎫
MARY ⎭ their children
GRANDMOTHER

Scene 1

The Brown family have come to the beach. Grandmother is walking between Mr and Mrs Brown. They are holding her arms. John and Mary are in front. They are looking for a place on the beach. John is carrying a chair. Mary has two baskets.

JOHN: Look, there's a nice place. Near the cliffs. (*They both go to it.*)

MARY: Yes, this is fine. (*They put down the chair and baskets. Mary calls to her mother and father.*) We've found a nice place near the cliffs. Be quick.

MRS BROWN: We can't come quickly. We can't leave your grandmother. You know she's old. She can't walk quickly.

GRANDMOTHER: I can walk by myself. I'm not a child!

MR BROWN: We'll stay with you, Grandmother. You may fall on these stones.

MRS BROWN: You have to take care at your age.

They reach the place near the cliffs at last.

MR BROWN: Yes, this will be all right. But don't leave the baskets there, Mary. Put them in the shade.

Mary puts the baskets in the shade.

JOHN: Shall I put Grandmother's chair in the shade, too?

MRS BROWN: No, not in the shade. Put it in the sun, John. Over there. (*She points to a place. It is a little way from the cliffs.*) The sun will be good for Grandmother.

GRANDMOTHER: But I don't want to sit in the sun! I want to read and have a little sleep.

I want to sit in the shade

MRS BROWN: Put the chair there, John. (*John takes the chair and puts it in the sun.*) That's right. Come along, Grandmother.

MR BROWN: Yes, come along. The sun will be good for you. We don't often have a warm day like this.

They lead Grandmother to the chair. Grandmother sits down.

MRS BROWN: There! It's nice in the sun, isn't it?

GRANDMOTHER: No, I want to sit in the shade. I told you. Can I have something to drink?

MRS BROWN: No, not yet. It's only three o'clock. We'll have tea at four.

Mr and Mrs Brown sit down near Grandmother's chair.

MARY: What are we going to do this afternoon? Are we going to stay here?

JOHN: Can we go in the sea?

MRS BROWN: No, not here, John. It isn't a good place.

JOHN (*to his father*): Can we go to the cave, then? You promised to take us there.

MRS BROWN: I'm tired. I want to have a rest. We can go later.

JOHN: No, we must go soon. The tide will come in. When the tide comes in, the cave is full of water.

MR BROWN: We ought to take them. I promised.

MRS BROWN: Where is the cave? Is it far?

MARY: It's about a mile from here.

MRS BROWN (*to her husband*): *You* take them, dear. I'll stay here and look after **Grandmother**.

GRANDMOTHER: Don't stay here for *me*. I can look after myself.

MARY: Oh, please come, Mummy. I don't want to go *without* you.

MRS BROWN: But what about Grandmother? We can't leave her here. She'll be all alone.

GRANDMOTHER: I *want* to be alone! I want to read and have a rest.

MRS BROWN: Are you sure, Grandmother? I don't like to leave you.

GRANDMOTHER: Yes, I'm quite sure. If you stay, you'll talk. I want to have a rest.

MRS BROWN: All right, Grandmother. (*She gets up. Mr Brown does the same.*) Here's your book. And your umbrella, too. Put up the umbrella if you feel warm.

Mr Brown and the children walk off. Mary calls to her mother.

MARY: Are you coming, Mum?

MRS BROWN: Yes, I'm ready. (*She turns to Grandmother.*) Goodbye, Grandmother. We'll soon be back. Then we'll have a nice cup of tea.

GRANDMOTHER: Goodbye. Have a nice time. (*She opens her book and begins to read it.*)

The Brown family walk across the beach.

GRANDMOTHER (*to herself*): Ah, they've gone at last! Now I'll move my chair into the shade. (*She puts her book on the sand. She stands up and carries her chair to the cliffs. She puts it behind a big rock. Then she sits down.*) Ah, it's nice behind this rock. I'm in the shade at last! Now I can have a good rest. (*She closes her eyes and is soon asleep.*)

Scene 2
The Brown family go into the cave.

MR BROWN: Well, here we are at last!

MRS BROWN: It's dark. I can't see a thing.

MR BROWN: Wait a minute. I've got a box of matches. I'll light one.

JOHN: Can I do it?

MR BROWN: No, you may drop the box.

Mr Brown lights a match. They can see the inside of the cave.

MR BROWN: How's that? *Now* you can see.

MARY: Here's a piece of paper. Light that, too.

Mr Brown lights the piece of paper.

MRS BROWN: It's cold and wet in here. I don't like it.

MARY: But it's a *famous* cave, Mummy.

Now you can see

MRS BROWN: Why, what happened here?

JOHN: Smugglers used to come here, didn't they?

MR BROWN: Yes, that's right. It was a smugglers' cave.

MRS BROWN: Did they live here? In this cave? It isn't a very nice place.

MARY: No, they didn't live here, Mummy. They used to bring things from the ships and hide them here.

The light goes out and the cave is dark again. Mr Brown lights a match.

JOHN: Can I go to the back of the cave? Let me have the matches, Dad.

MRS BROWN: No, stay here, John. You may fall. The floor of the cave is wet.

MARY: What did the smugglers do when the tide came in? Where did they put their things?

JOHN: There are some holes in the walls. They are higher than the water. The smugglers used to put their things there. Give me the matches, Dad, and I'll show you.

Mr Brown gives his son the box of matches. John goes to the back of the cave and lights a match.

JOHN: Can you see the holes. They're above my head.

MRS BROWN: Take care, John. You may fall.

At that moment John puts his foot in a hole. It is full of water. He drops the matches and the cave is dark again.

MRS BROWN: Now we're in the dark again.

MR BROWN: Have you got the matches, John?

JOHN: No, I've dropped them in the water.

MR BROWN: Then we'll have to go out. Come on, John.

MRS BROWN: I'm glad. I don't like this place.

Mrs Brown and Mary leave the cave. Mr Brown and John follow. They stand outside.

MR BROWN: Ah! It's nice to be outside again.

MRS BROWN: It's four o'clock. We've wasted almost an hour.

MARY: Oh look, the tide's coming in.

MR BROWN: Yes, it's come in a long way, hasn't it?

JOHN: It will soon reach the cave.

MARY (*pointing to the cliffs*): It's very near the cliffs.

MRS BROWN: Oh! What about Grandmother? We left her on the beach. Perhaps she's fallen asleep.

The tide's coming in

MR BROWN: I'm sure she's all right.
MRS BROWN: We ought to go back quickly.
JOHN: I'm going to run back. Come on, Mary.
The children run off. Mr and Mrs Brown follow them quickly.

Scene 3
Like **Scene 1**. *John and Mary arrive first.*

JOHN: She's not here.
MARY: Her chair's gone, too.
JOHN (*calling*): We can't see her, Dad.
Mr Brown reaches the place. Mrs Brown follows behind him.
MR BROWN: What's happened? Isn't Grandmother here?
MARY: We can't see her.
JOHN: She was there (*pointing*).
MARY: The tide's come in and covered that part.
MRS BROWN: We've lost her! (*She begins to cry.*)
MR BROWN: I can't believe it. The water isn't very deep.
MRS BROWN (*still crying*): Grandmother couldn't swim!

22

JOHN: Look, there's her book. In the sea!

MARY: And her umbrella.

MR BROWN: But where's her chair? I can't see that.

MRS BROWN: It's at the bottom of the sea. With grandmother on it. It's all my fault! She wanted to sit near the
cliffs, and I put her chair here.

MR BROWN: Don't cry, dear. It wasn't your fault.

JOHN: The tide's coming in quickly. Shall I get the baskets,
father?

MR BROWN: Yes, get the baskets. I'll look after your mother.

*John and Mary go to the big rock near the cliff. They both
begin to laugh.*

MR BROWN (*rather angrily*): Why are you children laughing?
We've lost your grandmother. This isn't the time to
laugh.

JOHN: Come and see, Dad.

*Mr and Mrs Brown go to the rock. Then they too begin to
laugh.*

Why, it's Grandmother

23

MRS BROWN: Why, it's Grandmother!

MR BROWN: And she's still asleep!

MARY: But how did she get here?

JOHN: And who carried her chair?

Grandmother hears their voices and wakes up.

GRANDMOTHER: Oh, you're back. Did you have a nice time? I've had a good sleep. What's the matter? Why are you all looking at me?

MARY: We couldn't find you, Grandmother.

JOHN: The tide has come in and we were afraid.

MR BROWN: We thought . . .

GRANDMOTHER (*laughing*): Well, I was here all the time.

MRS BROWN: But how did you get here?

GRANDMOTHER: I walked here of course.

MARY: But who carried your chair?

GRANDMOTHER: I carried it myself.

MRS BROWN (*beginning to get angry*): You carried it yourself! At your age! You oughtn't to do things like that, Grandmother. You'll get ill.

GRANDMOTHER: Well, I'm still alive! And now, what about tea?

MRS BROWN: Not yet. You'll have to wait.

GRANDMOTHER: But it's after four. I must have a cup of tea.

MRS BROWN: Later, Grandmother. The tide's coming in. We can't stop here.

MR BROWN: Bring the baskets, Mary. John, you can carry Grandmother's chair.

GRANDMOTHER (*getting up*): Don't forget my book and umbrella. I didn't bring them here.

MR BROWN: You've lost them. We saw them in the sea.

MRS BROWN: Yes, you've lost your umbrella. It was new. I bought it only last week.

MR BROWN: Well, it doesn't matter. We've still got Grandmother!

The Brown family begin to move off.

THE END

FRED'S OLD CAR

Characters

FRED YOUNG
EDNA BLACK, his girl-friend
MR BLACK
MRS BLACK
POLICEMAN
FIRST MAN
SECOND MAN

Scene 1

The sitting-room of the Blacks' house. It is Saturday afternoon. Edna is reading. Fred comes into the room. He is very excited.

EDNA: Hello, Fred. You look excited. What *is* it?

FRED: You'll never guess!

EDNA: Have you bought me a present?

FRED: It's a present for both of us.

EDNA: For both of us? I can't guess. Tell me.

FRED: I've bought a car!

EDNA: Oh, Fred! You've bought a car at last! Where is it?

FRED: It's standing outside the house. Go to the window and see.

Edna crosses to the window. Fred follows her. There are two cars outside the house. One is new. The second is very old.

EDNA (*looking at the new car*): It's beautiful, Fred.

FRED: I'm glad you like it.

EDNA: But it cost a lot of money, didn't it?

FRED: No, of course not. Old cars are very cheap.

EDNA: Oh, I was looking at the new car.

FRED: No, the *old* one is mine. You like it, don't you?

EDNA: Well, it doesn't look very nice.

FRED: That's not important. It's got a good engine. I drove it here and it went very well.

EDNA: But where did you get it?

I've bought a car!

FRED: I bought it from a friend. He's buying a new car, so he sold me his old one.

EDNA: He was glad to sell it! How much did you pay for it?

FRED: Only twenty-five pounds. It wasn't much.

EDNA: It's quite a lot of money. We want to *save* money, don't we?

FRED: I know. But we must have *some* pleasures. Come on, shall we go for a ride?

EDNA: I'm waiting for my father and mother. They're coming back for tea. (*Pointing out of the window.*) Look, there's their car now. You talk to them while I make the tea.

Edna goes out. After a few minutes Mr and Mrs Black come into the room.

MRS BLACK: Hello, Fred.

MR BLACK (*rather angrily*): I couldn't leave my car outside my own house! There are two cars there.

MRS BLACK: One is an ugly old car. It doesn't look nice outside the house.

MR BLACK: Who owns it?

FRED: It's mine.

MR BLACK (*surprised*): Yours? When did you buy a car?

FRED: Today. I'm sorry it's in the way.

MRS BLACK: But why did you buy an old car like that?

FRED: I need a car and I haven't much money.

MR BLACK: You've wasted your money, young man. You'll be sorry.

FRED: I know the car doesn't look nice. But it goes well.

MRS BLACK: For a few days perhaps. Then you'll have trouble.

MR BLACK: It's always the same with old cars. You ought to get a new one.

FRED: But I told you. I haven't enough money.

MR BLACK: You don't need a car. You can use mine when it's free.

MRS BLACK: Or you can come out with us.

FRED: We always go out in *your* car. Now we can go out in mine.

MRS BLACK: *I* won't!

They don't like it

Edna comes in with the tea.
EDNA: Has Fred told you about the car?
MRS BLACK: We've seen it!
FRED: They don't like it.
EDNA: Fred wants to go out for a ride. Will you come, too?
MRS BLACK: *I'm* not coming.
EDNA: Oh, mother, you must.
MR BLACK: Yes, we ought to give the car a chance. It looks
    ugly, but perhaps it goes well.
MRS BLACK: All right. But we won't go very far.
EDNA: Drink your tea, mother, and then we'll all go out.
They all sit down and drink their tea.

Scene 2

In the car. Fred is driving and Mr Black is sitting beside him. Edna and her mother are sitting in the back.

FRED (*rather excited*): You see! The car goes very well.

MRS BLACK: We haven't gone very far yet.

MR BLACK: The engine makes a lot of noise, doesn't it?

FRED: Well, it's not a *new* car, of course.

MRS BLACK: It smells, too. I think I shall be sick.

FRED: Open the window. Let the air come in.

MRS BLACK: It *is* open. You can't close it!

EDNA: You'll be all right when we reach the country, mother.

MR BLACK: Which way are we going?

FRED: Through the town.

MR BLACK: Is that a good idea, Fred? You haven't driven the car much.

EDNA: There are a lot of cars on the road. It's Saturday.

MRS BLACK: And a lot of people, too. I hope they don't see us.

FRED: They'll be busy. They won't look at *you*.

They reach the centre of the town. A policeman stops the line of cars. Fred is near the front of the line.

FRED: A lot of cars are crossing in front. We'll have to wait a few minutes.

MR BLACK: Turn off the engine, Fred. It's getting hot.

Fred turns off the engine.

EDNA: Look, there's Mrs Jones over there.

MR BLACK: She's looking at us.

MRS BLACK: I'm not surprised. She'll tell all her friends about the car and they'll have a good laugh.

FRED: Let them laugh. What does it matter?

MR BLACK: The traffic is moving again. You can go now.

Fred turns on the engine. The car moves a little way and then stops.

MR BLACK: What's the matter?

FRED: I don't know. The car won't move.

MRS BLACK: It's a fine place to stop! In the middle of the road!

EDNA: The policeman is coming across, Fred.

POLICEMAN: Are you in trouble, sir? What's the matter?

29

FRED: I'm not sure. The car won't go.

POLICEMAN: Well, you can't stop here. The cars can't go past. We'll push the car to the side of the road.

Fred gets out. They push the car to the side of the road. Then they open the front of the car and look at the engine.

POLICEMAN: The engine's very dirty. Perhaps that's the trouble.

FRED: It was running very well. I can't understand it.

POLICEMAN: Have you got enough petrol in the car, sir? People often forget to put in petrol.

FRED: Oh, I didn't think about that. (*He looks inside the car.*)

POLICEMAN: Well?

FRED: I'm afraid you're right. I haven't any petrol.

POLICEMAN: Hm. You ought to think of these things.

FRED: I'm very sorry. Where can I get some petrol?

POLICEMAN: There's a garage down the road. (*He walks off.*)

MRS BLACK: What are we going to do now?

FRED: I'll go to the garage and get some petrol.

The engine's very dirty

MRS BLACK: We have to sit here and wait! Oh, why did I come? It was a great mistake.

MR BLACK: Next time we'll go in *my* car.

Fred goes to the garage. Mr and Mrs Black and Edna sit in the car. A big car goes slowly past them and then stops. Two men get out and walk back to Fred's car.

FIRST MAN (*looking at Fred's car*): What do you think, Henry?

SECOND MAN: I can't believe my eyes.

FIRST MAN: It's the right car.

SECOND MAN: It's in good condition, too.

FIRST MAN: You're right. It will need a little paint. That's all.

SECOND MAN: So we've found the car at last.

MRS BLACK (*to her husband*): Why are those two men looking at the car? What do they want?

EDNA: Ask them, father.

MR BLACK (*putting his head out of the window*): Can I help you?

SECOND MAN (*coming to the car*): I'm sorry, sir. I ought to explain. My name's Henry North. Here's my card. (*He gives his card to Mr Black.*)

FIRST MAN: I'm sure you know the name. Mr North makes films.

EDNA: Yes, he's famous, father. I've seen all his films.

MR BLACK: But why were you looking at the car? You haven't told us the reason.

SECOND MAN: I'll explain. We're going to make a film about old cars and we want one like this. It's rather a special kind. They only made a few like this and today it is hard to find one.

FIRST MAN: We've looked for a long time but we couldn't find a good one.

MR BLACK: I see. So you want to use this car in a film.

FIRST MAN: That's the idea.

SECOND MAN: Do you want to sell it? We'll give you a good price, of course.

MR BLACK: Well, it isn't my car.

MRS BLACK: But I'm sure you can have it.

Can I help you?

EDNA: Wait a minute, mother. It's Fred's car, not yours.

SECOND MAN: Who is Fred?

EDNA: He's my boy-friend. He's gone to the garage for some petrol.

MR BLACK: He'll be back in a moment.

FIRST MAN: So you stopped here because you hadn't any petrol. That was a good thing for us!

EDNA: Here's Fred now.

Fred arrives with the petrol. He looks at the two men.

FRED: What's all this? Are we in trouble again?

EDNA (*laughing*): You'll never guess. These two men want to buy your car.

FRED: But I don't want to sell it.

MRS BLACK: But Fred! They want to use it in a film.

SECOND MAN: Let me explain, sir. We need a car like yours. We'll buy it from you if you like. Or you can let us use it and we'll pay you.

EDNA: You can't say no, Fred. Think! Your car will be

Here's Fred now

famous. It will appear in a film.

FRED: Well, I don't want to sell it. But you can certainly use it.

SECOND MAN: Good! And we'll pay you well.

FIRST MAN: Give us your name and address, sir. We want to make the film quite soon. We'll write to you when we are ready.

Fred gives his name and address to the men. They go back to their car and drive off. Fred puts the petrol in the car and gets in.

FRED: Perhaps we ought to go home now. I must take good care of the car.

EDNA: Fred's right. He oughtn't to use the car much before they make the film.

MRS BLACK: No, Fred promised to take us for a ride and he must.

EDNA: Mother likes the car now!

MRS BLACK: When I see Mrs Jones, I'll tell her about the film. She won't laugh then!

They drive off.

THE END

Look at that picture over there

THE NEW ASSISTANT

Characters

MR HIGGINS, owner of the shop
TOM, the new assistant
FIRST CUSTOMER
SECOND CUSTOMER
YOUNG MAN
YOUNG WOMAN
RICH LADY

Scene 1

A shop. It is full of old things: pictures, pots, plates and some furniture. It is Tom's first morning in the shop. Mr Higgins is explaining the business to him.

MR HIGGINS: It takes a long time to learn about these old things. I've sold them all my life, but I still make mistakes.

TOM: Well, *I* don't want to make mistakes.

MR HIGGINS (*picking up a silver pot*): This silver pot, for example.

TOM: It looks quite nice.

MR HIGGINS: I paid ten pounds for it. But it's only worth about seven pounds. It isn't very good silver. I made a mistake when I bought it.

TOM: I see. What price will you get for it?

MR HIGGINS: Perhaps eight pounds. So I'll lose two pounds. But look at that picture over there. (*He points to a picture.*)

TOM: The big one, near the window?

MR HIGGINS: That's the one. Well, I paid only fifteen pounds for it, but I'll sell it for twenty-five.

TOM: A profit of ten pounds. That's quite good.

MR HIGGINS: Yes, it's not bad. But remember, some things in the shop are worth a hundred pounds.

TOM: But how can I know the price? I can't be sure.

MR HIGGINS: I'll tell you, of course. I don't want to lose money!

35

TOM: But you may not be here. What shall I do then?

MR HIGGINS: I've thought of that. I've marked the price in very small numbers. You can try to get a *bigger* price. The customer won't see the numbers.

TOM: I'm beginning to understand.

MR HIGGINS: For example, I've marked the price behind the picture. Twenty-five pounds. And I've marked it under this pot. Pick it up and have a look.

TOM (*picking up the silver pot*): Yes, here's the price. Eight pounds. But I can try to sell it for nine.

MR HIGGINS: That's the right idea! You're learning quickly! Yes, ask for nine pounds and perhaps you'll get eight. That's business.

TOM: But perhaps the customer will only offer six.

MR HIGGINS: That's not enough. But he may buy two or three things. Then you can sell it for six. Do you understand the idea?

TOM: Yes. I mustn't lose money.

MR HIGGINS: That's right. If you lose money, you're not the right assistant for *me*.

TOM: But you'll be in the shop today, won't you?

MR HIGGINS: I have to go out for a short time. For about an hour. But it's all right. Remember, I've marked the price on things. If you're not sure, don't sell.

TOM: All right. I'll take care.

MR HIGGINS: Look, there's a man outside the shop now. He's coming in. Listen to me and you'll learn something.

The man comes into the shop.

MR HIGGINS: Good morning, sir.

FIRST CUSTOMER: Good morning. I wanted to look round your shop.

MR HIGGINS: Yes, of course, sir. Are you looking for something special? Are you interested in pictures, for example?

FIRST CUSTOMER: No, not pictures. But I'm interested in glass things.

MR HIGGINS: Glass? I have a few good pieces of glass. Allow me to show you, sir. (*He takes out some pieces of glass and puts them in front of the man.*) Do you like any of these?

The man picks up two or three pieces and looks at them.

This vase is rather nice

FIRST CUSTOMER: This vase is rather nice.

MR HIGGINS: Yes, it is, isn't it? It's quite an old piece. I haven't many pieces like that.

FIRST CUSTOMER: My wife likes glass things. I'm looking for a present for her.

MR HIGGINS: Well, she'll certainly like this.

FIRST CUSTOMER: How much is it?

MR HIGGINS: Three pounds, sir. Not much for a vase like this.

FIRST CUSTOMER: I know. But I didn't want to spend three pounds.

MR HIGGINS: All right. You can have it for two pounds 75p. I paid two pounds 50p for it. I must make a small profit, mustn't I?

FIRST CUSTOMER: That's a fair price. All right. I'll take it.

MR HIGGINS: You won't be sorry, sir. Your wife will like it.

Mr Higgins puts the vase in some paper. The customer pays Mr Higgins and takes the vase.

MR HIGGINS: Thank you, sir. Perhaps we'll see you again.

These numbers are not very clear

FIRST CUSTOMER: Yes, I'll come in if I'm near your shop. Good morning.

MR HIGGINS: Good morning, sir.

The customer goes out. Mr Higgins and Tom are alone in the shop.

MR HIGGINS: Well, do you understand the idea?

TOM: Yes, but you didn't make much profit. Only 25 pence.

MR HIGGINS: Of course I did. I made quite a good profit.

TOM: But you paid £2.50 for the vase.

MR HIGGINS: Oh, I *said* that. But in fact I paid £1.50. So I made a profit of £1.25. That's not bad, is it?

TOM: It's very good.

MR HIGGINS: And *you* must do the same, young man. Well, I'm going out now. I'll be back before twelve. Remember, if you're not sure, don't sell.

TOM: I won't forget, Mr Higgins.

Mr Higgins puts on his hat and coat and goes out.

Scene 2

Tom is alone in the shop. He walks round and picks up certain things. He wants to learn the prices.

TOM (*looking under a vase*): Hm. These numbers are not very clear. Let me see. How much does this cost? (*He looks behind a picture.*) Twelve pounds fifty pence. I hope that I don't make any mistakes!

The door opens and a second customer comes in.

TOM: Good morning, sir. Can I help you?

SECOND CUSTOMER: Mr Higgins isn't in, is he?

TOM: No, he had to go out. I'm his new assistant. Did you want to see Mr Higgins?

SECOND CUSTOMER (*quickly*): Oh no, that's all right. I'm interested in that picture. (*He points to the big picture near the window.*)

TOM: Ah, that one, sir! Yes, that's a very good picture. Mr Higgins was telling me about it.

SECOND CUSTOMER: Was he? What did he say?

I'm interested in that picture

39

TOM: He said it was a good picture. It's worth a lot of money.

SECOND CUSTOMER: I see. How much does he want for it?

TOM: You can have it for twenty-seven pounds.

SECOND CUSTOMER: Twenty-seven pounds? For that picture?

TOM: Twenty-six, then. That's my last offer.

SECOND CUSTOMER (*in an angry voice*): Why, he robbed me!

TOM: I don't understand, sir. Who robbed you?

SECOND CUSTOMER: Mr Higgins, of course. I sold him that picture. He gave me fifteen pounds for it. And now he's selling it for twenty-six. I won't sell *him* a picture again.

The man goes out of the shop. He closes the door with a lot of noise.

TOM (*to himself*): That won't please Mr Higgins. But how could I know?

A young man and woman come into the shop.

TOM: Good morning. Can I help you? Are you looking for something special?

YOUNG MAN: Yes, we wanted to look at some rings.

TOM: With pleasure, sir. We have a few rings. I'll show them to you.

Tom puts some rings in front of them.

YOUNG MAN (*to the woman*): Have a look at these, dear. Do you like any of them?

YOUNG WOMAN (*picking up two or three rings*): They're all rather heavy. Ah, here's a nice one.

YOUNG MAN: Yes, it's nice, isn't it? Put it on, dear.

The young woman puts the ring on her finger.

TOM: It's very good silver, madam.

YOUNG WOMAN: I like it, but it's rather big. (*She takes it off.*)

YOUNG MAN (*picking up a different ring*): What about this one?

YOUNG WOMAN (*putting it on*): Yes, I like this one. My sister's got a ring like this.

YOUNG MAN: And it's the right size. We'll take it if you like it.

YOUNG WOMAN: But what's the price?

YOUNG MAN (*to Tom*): How much does it cost?

TOM: There's a small card on the ring. Let me see. (*The*

I like it

woman gives Tom the ring.) Yes, twelve pounds.

YOUNG WOMAN: It's a lot of money. Have we got enough?

YOUNG MAN: Of course. If you like it, I'll buy it for you.

YOUNG WOMAN (*to Tom*): Can we have it for eleven?

TOM: I'm sorry, madam. I can't change the price. I'm only the assistant.

YOUNG MAN: It's all right. We'll take it. (*He takes twelve pounds from his pocket and gives it to Tom.*)

TOM: Thank you, sir.

YOUNG WOMAN (*to young man*): Thank you, dear. It's a beautiful present. (*She puts the ring on her finger.*)

YOUNG MAN: I'm glad you like it. (*To Tom.*) Thank you. Good morning.

TOM: Thank you, sir. Good morning. Come again!

The young man and woman go out of the shop.

TOM (*to himself*): Well, that wasn't bad. I didn't make a profit, but I didn't lose any money. Perhaps I'll make a profit next time!

After a time the next customer comes in. She is wearing very good clothes and is clearly rich.

TOM: Good morning, madam. Can I help you?

RICH LADY: Good morning. I want to see some pictures. Have you got any good ones?

TOM: Yes, madam. Do you like that one? (*He points to the big picture.*) Near the window.

RICH LADY (*going to the picture*): Yes, it's rather nice. How much does it cost?

TOM (*thinking quickly*): Well, the price is thirty pounds, but you can have it for twenty-eight.

RICH LADY: Twenty-eight. No, I'll give you twenty-seven for it.

TOM: All right, madam. Do you want to take it or shall I send it?

RICH LADY: I'll take it. I have my car outside.

TOM: I'll put some paper round it. It'll take a few minutes. Please look round the shop.

The rich lady walks round the shop. She stops in front of a large blue vase. It is very ugly.

RICH LADY: Oh, I like this. It's very old, isn't it?

TOM (*quickly*): Yes, Mr Higgins said it was old. He knows about these things. It's Chinese.

RICH LADY: It's rather ugly. But I like ugly things.

TOM: Different people have different tastes, madam.

RICH LADY: How much is it?

TOM: I'll have a look. (*He picks up the vase and looks under it. The numbers are not very clear, so he takes it to the window.*) Ah yes, one hundred and ten pounds. Quite a lot of money! Of course you don't often see Chinese vases like this.

RICH LADY: A hundred and ten pounds. Well, it may be worth it, but I don't want to pay that price. I'll give you a hundred pounds for it.

TOM: I can't take off ten pounds, madam. I'm only the assistant here. I'm not the owner of the shop. But you can have it for a hundred and five pounds.

RICH LADY: No, a hundred. It may be worth only ninety. Who knows?

TOM: Mr Higgins put the prices on these things, madam. He

42

Ah yes, £110

understands their value. Perhaps you can call again and see Mr Higgins. He may take a hundred.

RICH LADY: No, I'm a very busy person. I don't often come to this part of town. Are you sure you can't take a hundred?

TOM: I'm sorry, madam.

RICH LADY: Well, it doesn't matter. I've saved a hundred pounds. Will you bring the picture to my car?

TOM: Of course, madam. With pleasure.

The woman pays Tom for the picture and goes out of the shop. Tom takes the picture to the car and comes back.

TOM (*to himself*): Let me see. How have I done this morning? I sold the ring for the right price and I made two pounds on the picture. I didn't sell the vase, but perhaps the woman will come back. I hope this will please Mr Higgins.

Scene 3

Later that morning. Mr Higgins has come back to the shop.

MR HIGGINS: Well, young man, how have you done? What

have you sold this morning?

TOM: Well, first I had some trouble about that big picture.

MR HIGGINS: Ah, but you've sold it.

TOM: Yes, but not to that person.

MR HIGGINS: What happened?

TOM: A man came into the shop and asked the price of the picture. When I told him, he got very angry.

MR HIGGINS: But why? How much did you ask?

TOM: I asked for twenty-seven pounds.

MR HIGGINS: That's all right. The picture was worth twenty-five.

TOM: But he sold *you* the picture and you only paid him fifteen pounds. He said you robbed him!

MR HIGGINS: Oh, the same man! Well, it doesn't matter. It wasn't your fault.

TOM: Then a young man and woman came in.

MR HIGGINS: Did they buy the picture?

TOM: No, they bought a ring. They paid twelve pounds for it. I got the right price for it.

MR HIGGINS: Good.

TOM: Then a rich lady came to the shop.

MR HIGGINS: And she bought the picture. How much did you get for it?

TOM: Twenty-seven pounds. I asked for twenty-eight, but she only wanted to pay twenty-seven. So I accepted it.

MR HIGGINS: Good! Good! That's a profit of twelve pounds. You're learning quickly! Did she buy only the picture?

TOM: Yes, that was all. Oh, she also wanted that blue vase.

MR HIGGINS: The ugly one? Why didn't you sell it to her? It doesn't cost much.

TOM: But the price is rather high. It's Chinese, isn't it?

MR HIGGINS: No, of course not. I can't remember the price, but it doesn't cost much. (*He goes to the vase and looks under it.*) Yes, one pound ten pence. You said that she was rich. One pound ten isn't much money!

TOM: One pound ten pence? Are you sure? (*He looks at the price on the vase.*) Yes, you're quite right.

MR HIGGINS: Of course I'm right. Why, how much did you ask for it?

Yes, £1.10

TOM: I asked for a hundred and ten pounds.

MR HIGGINS (*laughing*): A hundred and ten pounds! For that ugly old vase! Well, of course she didn't want to pay that.

TOM: No, but she offered me a hundred pounds.

MR HIGGINS: Is this a joke? (*He is not laughing now.*)

TOM: No, it isn't a joke, Mr Higgins. She offered me a hundred pounds.

MR HIGGINS: And you didn't take it?

TOM: Well, no, sir. I thought that it was worth a hundred and ten pounds. I asked for one hundred and five, but she didn't want to pay that. I didn't want to lose money, sir.

MR HIGGINS (*very angry*): You didn't want to lose money! You've lost nearly a hundred pounds. I have sold old things for forty years, and no one has offered me a hundred pounds for an old vase. And you said NO!

TOM: I'm very sorry, Mr Higgins.

MR HIGGINS: . . . !

THE END

45

This coffee has a terrible taste

A BAD DREAM

Characters

GEORGE HILL, the manager of a bank
JANE HILL, his wife
ANNIE, their cook
MR BRIGGS, the assistant manager of the bank
MR WINTER, the cashier

Scene 1

It is about two o'clock on Sunday afternoon. Mr and Mrs Hill have had lunch and they are drinking coffee in the sitting-room.

MR HILL: Ugh! This coffee has a terrible taste. Why can't Annie make good coffee? It's quite easy. You can show her.

MRS HILL: I *have* shown her. You know that. She makes good coffee for a few days, and then she forgets again. I'm afraid she isn't very clever.

MR HILL: You're quite right. She *isn't* very clever. And she's a bad cook. The lunch was terrible, too. I wanted to talk to you about it.

MRS HILL: Must you do it now? It's Sunday afternoon.

MR HILL: No, it can't wait. I must speak to you about Annie.

MRS HILL (*rather sadly*): All right. Tell me.

MR HILL: Well, the trouble is this. People come to our house. They come for dinner and they get bad food. What do these people think of me? *I'm* their bank manager.

MRS HILL: But what can I do, George? I know the food isn't very good. Next time I'll cook the dinner myself.

MR HILL: No, you can't do that. You're my wife and you must meet these people. You can't spend your time in the kitchen.

MRS HILL: What is the answer, then?

MR HILL: It's easy. We must get a new cook.

MRS HILL: But Annie has been with us for a long time, George. Nearly twenty years. We can't do this to her. She

47

isn't a young woman now. How will she find a new job?

MR HILL: I don't know. She must go. Things are different now. I'm the manager of a big bank. We must have a good cook.

MRS HILL: *You're* different now, George. You've changed. You don't care about people.

MR HILL: I care about the bank. And I care about our customers. So Annie must go. Explain the matter to her. She'll understand. Give her three months. She can find a new job in that time.

MRS HILL: It won't be easy.

MR HILL: Will you tell her today?

MRS HILL: Can't I do it tomorrow?

MR HILL: No, you'll forget about it. Do it today.

MRS HILL: All right. I'll speak to her today. Poor woman!

MR HILL: I feel rather tired. I think I'll have a little sleep.

MRS HILL (*getting up*): You stay here. I have something to do. I won't disturb you.

Mrs Hill goes out of the room. Mr Hill puts his feet on a chair and closes his eyes. He is soon asleep.

I'll have a little sleep

Scene 2

Mr Hill is still asleep. There is a knock at the door. Mr Hill hears the knock and wakes up.

MR HILL (*calling out*): Who's there? Come in.

Two men come into the room. The first is Briggs, the assistant manager of the bank. The second is Winter, the cashier.

BRIGGS: Good afternoon, sir. We're not disturbing you, are we?

MR HILL: Why, it's Briggs! And Winter! In fact I was having a little sleep. What is it? Is it something important?

BRIGGS: It *is* rather important, sir.

MR HILL: I hope it isn't trouble. The bank isn't on fire, is it?

Mr Hill laughs at his joke. Briggs and Winter do not laugh.

BRIGGS: No, sir, the bank isn't on fire. But we had to see you. We want to talk to you.

MR HILL: Today? It's Sunday. Can't it wait? You can tell me tomorrow. Come and see me in my office.

WINTER: It can't wait, sir. We must talk to you today.

MR HILL: I don't understand. Well, sit down, both of you. (*The two men sit down.*) Now, what's the matter?

BRIGGS: It's not easy to begin, sir.

WINTER: Shall I tell him, Briggs? One of us must do it.

BRIGGS: No, *I'll* do it. I'm the assistant manager. Well, sir, we think you ought to resign.

MR HILL (*in a very surprised voice*): Resign? Leave the bank? What are you talking about? Is this a joke, Briggs?

BRIGGS: No, it isn't a joke.

MR HILL (*sitting up in his chair*): Now one minute, please. It's Sunday afternoon. You come to my house and disturb me. Then you tell me . . . that I ought to resign.

WINTER: We're very sorry, sir. We know it's Sunday. But we had to tell you.

MR HILL: But you can't do this. I'm the manager. You're only the assistant manager, Briggs. And Winter is only the cashier. You can't speak to me like this.

BRIGGS: We're doing it for the bank, sir.

WINTER: It will be a good thing for the bank, sir. Believe me.

MR HILL (*standing up*): I've had enough! Go home, both of you. Take a holiday tomorrow. You both need a rest.

BRIGGS: We're all right, sir. We don't need a holiday.

WINTER: But we *must* have your answer today, sir. Will you resign?

MR HILL (*sitting down again*): It's like a bad dream! Why must I resign? What have I done? Tell me that.

BRIGGS: You don't manage the bank well, sir.

MR HILL: (*angrily*): Of course I manage the bank well. Thousands of people use our bank. Business is very good.

BRIGGS: Oh, we know that, sir. But *we* do all the work. They use our bank because *we* work hard.

WINTER: And you're not nice to the people in the bank. You're nice to the customers, but not to us. No one likes you!

MR HILL: Oh, I know they don't like me. They have to work hard, and they don't like that.

WINTER: But *you* don't work hard, sir.

Of course I manage the bank well

MR HILL: Of course I do.

BRIGGS: Oh, no, sir. For example, you come late in the morning.

WINTER: And you often leave early.

BRIGGS: And you take two or three hours for lunch. We spend all day in the bank, but *you* are never there!

MR HILL: But I'm the manager. That's part of my job. I have to look after important people. I have to have lunch with them. It's good business.

BRIGGS: It's pleasure, sir! You're very fond of good food.

MR HILL: I won't listen to this.

WINTER: But you must.

MR HILL: I shall write to the head office about you. Then *you* will have to resign.

BRIGGS: We've already written about *you*, sir.

WINTER: Yes, sir. We explained the matter and they agree with us.

MR HILL: What! You've written to the head office. Behind my back!

BRIGGS: We had to do it, sir. We were only thinking of the bank.

WINTER: And they agree you must resign.

MR HILL: But they can't do this to me! I've spent thirty years in the bank.

BRIGGS: Think of the bank, sir. It will be a happier place without you!

MR HILL: But what am I going to do? I'm not a young man. How can I find a new job?

WINTER: Oh, you'll find something, sir. A job in an office.

BRIGGS: And you can have time, sir. Two or three months. You'll be able to find a new job.

MR HILL: I'm not sure.

BRIGGS: But you promise to resign, don't you, sir?

MR HILL: Well, I must. The head office agrees with you.

WINTER: Thank you, sir.

BRIGGS: We're sorry about this, sir.

Briggs and Winter stand up.

BRIGGS: You'll come to the office tomorrow, won't you, sir?

MR HILL: Er—yes, I'll be there.

WINTER: But please come on time, sir.

Briggs and Winter say good afternoon and go out. Mr Hill sits with his head in his hands. After a time Mrs Hill comes in. She is wearing a heavy coat and she has a bag in her hand.

MR HILL (*looking up*): Oh, it's you, dear. Briggs and Winter were here. They left a short time ago.

MRS HILL: Yes, I saw them when they were going out.

MR HILL: They came to tell me something. It isn't very pleasant. (*After a moment.*) I have to resign from the bank.

MRS HILL: Yes, I know.

MR HILL (*surprised*): Do you know already?

MRS HILL: Yes, they told me.

MR HILL: They couldn't wait! Did they tell you the reason, too?

MRS HILL: Yes, the people in the bank don't like you. I'm not very surprised.

MR HILL: I've spent all my life in the bank and now I've lost my job.

Mr Hill notices that his wife is wearing a coat.

MR HILL: Oh, are you going out? (*He sees the bag too.*) And

Are you going out?

you've got a bag. Where are you going?

MRS HILL: I need a holiday. I'm going to spend a few days with my sister.

MR HILL: At this time? But I need your help now.

MRS HILL: I can't help you. And I must have a holiday. I can't wait.

MR HILL: But you can have a holiday later. We'll go together.

MRS HILL: Where will you get the money for a holiday? You've lost your job. It won't be easy to find a new one. You're not a young man.

MR HILL: I've got three months. I'll find something.

MRS HILL: I hope you're right.

MR HILL: You're leaving me because I'm in trouble. When are you coming back?

MRS HILL: I have no idea. I'll write and let you know.

MR HILL: But who's going to look after me?

MRS HILL: There's Annie. Speak to her nicely and perhaps she'll stay. Well, goodbye, George. Write to me when you have a job.

Mrs Hill goes out of the room.

MR HILL (*to himself*): This is a terrible afternoon! I've lost my job and now my wife has gone too!

There is a knock at the door and Annie comes in.

MR HILL: What is it, Annie? Do you want to leave, too?

ANNIE: Leave, sir? I came about the tea, sir. It's almost four o'clock. Shall I bring tea, sir?

MR HILL: So you don't want to leave. Are you sure?

ANNIE: No, of course not, sir. I'm very happy here.

MR HILL: I've lost my job. Did you know that?

ANNIE: Yes, sir, Mrs Hill told me.

MR HILL: And my wife has gone for a long holiday.

ANNIE: I know, sir. But she'll come back. I'll look after you while she isn't here.

MR HILL: I won't have much money. Perhaps I won't be able to pay you.

ANNIE: It doesn't matter, sir. I've saved some money, so I don't need any now. But I want to stay here, sir. It's my home.

Do you want to leave too?

MR HILL: Thank you, Annie.

ANNIE: Shall I bring tea now, sir?

MR HILL: Later, please. In about half an hour.

ANNIE: Very well, sir.

Annie goes out. Mr Hill puts his feet on the chair again and closes his eyes.

Scene 3

Mrs Hill comes into the room. Her husband is still asleep.

MRS HILL: George! It's almost half past four.

MR HILL (*waking up*): What's that? Half past four? Oh, it's you, dear.

MRS HILL: Yes, of course it's me.

MR HILL: Then you haven't gone to your sister's.

MRS HILL: What *are* you talking about? I haven't been out of the house. You've been asleep all the afternoon.

MR HILL: Have I? Then I was dreaming. (*He remembers*

54

the dream.) It wasn't a very pleasant dream.

MRS HILL: You must tell me about it. Shall we have tea now?

MR HILL: That's a good idea. I need a cup of tea!

Mrs Hill rings the bell for Annie.

MR HILL: By the way, dear. Have you spoken to Annie yet?

MRS HILL: No, not yet. Give me a chance. I've been busy.
But I haven't forgotten. I'll tell her this evening.

MR HILL: I was thinking about it again. Perhaps we ought
to keep her. She's been with us a long time. And she may
not get a new job.

MRS HILL: I told you that, dear!

Shall I bring tea now, madam?

MR HILL: I agree with you now. Of course she isn't a good
cook, but she works hard.

MRS HILL: Yes, she works very hard.

MR HILL: Perhaps she needs help in the house. We can get
someone.

MRS HILL: That's a nice idea. Annie will like that. But what about your dinners? Who will cook when your friends come?

MR HILL: Oh, the dinners aren't important. We won't ask people very often.

MRS HILL: I'm glad. I never liked those dinners. (*After a moment.*) But, George, why have you changed suddenly? You're quite different now!

MR HILL: Am I? I'm glad you say that.

MRS HILL: Was it your dream? You must tell me about it.

MR HILL: No, I don't want to talk about it. But I won't forget it!

Annie comes into the room.

ANNIE: Shall I bring tea now, madam?

THE END

THE PROFESSOR

Characters

PROFESSOR HUNTER, an old man
MARY HUNTER, his daughter
MISS GREEN, his secretary
DR FITT ⎱ the men from London
ROSE ⎰
INSPECTOR HADLEY
SERGEANT BULL

Scene 1

Mary Hunter and Miss Green are in the professor's room. It is a large, pleasant room, with a lot of books in it. There is a big desk near the window.

MARY: Father's very excited this morning, Miss Green. He didn't want his breakfast. He only had a cup of coffee.

MISS GREEN: Yes, of course he's excited. I'm rather excited, too. This is a very important day. He is ready to give his invention to the world. Of course he hasn't built the machine, but the papers are complete. I copied them myself.

MARY: But what *is* his invention? I know it's a machine. But that's all. Father tried to explain it to me but I couldn't understand. Do you understand it?

MISS GREEN: No, not very well! Only the professor *really* understands it. But I know it's good. The government likes the idea. Your father wants to give his invention to the government. He wants to help people.

MARY: Yes, I'm sorry Father can't go to London himself. He wanted to go, of course, but he's not very strong. So the men from the government are coming here. They'll take the papers to London.

MISS GREEN: And then the professor will be famous!

The telephone rings. Miss Green picks it up and answers.

But what is his invention?

MISS GREEN: Hello? Yes, this is Professor Hunter's house. Yes, Miss Hunter is here. One moment, please. (*She gives the telephone to Mary Hunter.*) It's for you, dear. I think it's Dr Smith.

MARY: Good morning. Miss Hunter speaking. Yes, Dr Smith, I'm very well, thank you. Yes, Father's well, too. He's excited this morning, but we'll look after him. What's that? Freda's in hospital? Yes, of course I'll come. I wanted to stay with Father, but it doesn't matter. Yes, I'll be there in an hour. Goodbye.

Mary Hunter puts the telephone down.

MISS GREEN: What's the matter with your friend? Is she very ill?

MARY: She's broken her leg and they've taken her to hospital. She's asked to see me, so I must go. Oh dear! I wanted to stay here this morning. I wanted to look after Father.

MISS GREEN: It's all right, Mary. *I'll* be with him. I *am* his secretary.

The professor comes into the room. He cannot see well because he is old.

PROFESSOR: I can't find my glasses. (*To Mary.*) Have you seen them?

MISS GREEN (*going to the professor's desk*): Here they are, professor. (*She gives the glasses to the professor.*)

PROFESSOR: Ah, thank you, Miss Green. (*He puts on his glasses.*) I can't see without them. Now, what's the time? Hm, where's my watch? (*He looks for his watch in his pocket.*)

MARY (*laughing*): You're wearing it, Father. I bought you a new one. Don't you remember?

PROFESSOR (*also laughing*): Yes, of course you did. I quite forgot. I forget a lot of things, don't I? But I can still do my work! That's the important thing.

MARY: Of course it is, Father.

PROFESSOR (*looking at his watch*): Why, it's almost ten. When are the men coming from London? (*To Miss Green.*) At ten thirty, wasn't it?

MISS GREEN: No, eleven.

I can't find my glasses

PROFESSOR: Oh, I thought it was ten thirty. It doesn't matter. I can read through my papers again.

MARY: Dr Smith telephoned a few minutes ago, father.

PROFESSOR: Oh, what did he want?

MARY: My friend Freda's broken her leg and they've taken her to hospital. She asked to see me. So I have to leave now. I'm sorry I can't stay with you.

PROFESSOR: That's all right, Mary. Miss Green will look after me.

MARY: I must go, then. I'll be back at twelve. You can tell me about your morning.

PROFESSOR: Goodbye, dear. Give my love to Freda.

Mary kisses her father and goes out.

PROFESSOR: Now, let me see. Ah yes, my papers. (*He goes to his desk and sits down.*)

MISS GREEN: Do you need me now, professor?

PROFESSOR: Er, no. I want to be alone. I'll ring if I need you.

Miss Green goes out of the room.

PROFESSOR (*talking to himself*): Hm, these women! They

think I can't look after myself. I may lose my glasses.
I may forget about my watch. But these things aren't
important. (*He begins to read his papers.*)

Scene 2

*Half an hour later. The professor is still reading his papers.
Miss Green comes into the room.*

MISS GREEN (*very excited*): They're here, professor! They've
    arrived!

PROFESSOR (*looking up*): Who, Miss Green? What are you
    talking about?

MISS GREEN: The men from the government, of course.

PROFESSOR (*looking at his watch*): But it's only half past ten.
    You said they were coming at eleven.

MISS GREEN: Well, they've come early. Shall I bring them
    in or must they wait?

PROFESSOR: No, no, bring them in of course. But give me
    five minutes. I want to finish this page.

Miss Green goes to the door. Then she stops.

MISS GREEN: Oh, they've shown me their cards, professor.
    They *are* the right men.

PROFESSOR: Good. I wanted to see their cards, but it won't
    be necessary now. I don't want to give my invention to
    the wrong men!

*Miss Green goes out. After five minutes she comes in again. The
two men are with her.*

DR FITT: Good morning, professor. My name's Fitt. Dr Fitt.
    And this is Mr Rose. He's my assistant. He's . . . looking
    after me. We don't want to lose your papers!

PROFESSOR: Lose my papers? Oh, I see. No, of course not.
    Well, please sit down.

*Miss Green puts two chairs near the professor's desk and the
two men sit down.*

MISS GREEN: Shall I bring some coffee?

DR FITT: No coffee for us, thank you. We can't stay long. We
    have to go back to London soon.

Miss Green goes out.

PROFESSOR: So you've come for my papers. For my inven-
    tion.

DR FITT: That's right, professor.

My name's Fitt and this is Mr Rose

PROFESSOR: I wanted to go to London myself, but my daughter didn't let me go.

DR FITT: I'm sorry, professor. But we'll take care of the papers.

PROFESSOR: Now let me see. Where did I put them?

Dr Fitt is rather surprised. He looks at Mr Rose.

DR FITT: There are some papers on your desk, professor. Are they the ones?

PROFESSOR: Oh, these? No, they're not the papers for you. These are only some old papers. Ah, I remember now. I put the papers behind some books. (*He stands up.*)

DR FITT: Behind your books? That's not a very good place for papers, is it?

PROFESSOR: Yes, it is. No one touches my books. (*He takes down some books. There are some papers behind them.*) Yes, here they are. (*He gives the papers to Dr Fitt.*) You know about my invention, don't you?

DR FITT: Why, of course. We've talked about it in the office.

PROFESSOR: I see.

DR FITT (*looking at the papers*): Yes, the government thinks your invention is very important. It's going to help the world. You'll be famous, professor.

PROFESSOR: I don't want to be famous. I only want to help people. So I'm giving my invention to the government. I don't want any money for it.

Yes, here they are

DR FITT: Yes, we understand that, sir. The country will thank you for it. (*He looks at his watch.*) I'm afraid we have to go now.

PROFESSOR: Well, take good care of the papers.

Dr Fitt puts the papers in his bag and stands up. Mr Rose stands up, too.

DR FITT: Well, goodbye, professor. We'll write to you.

PROFESSOR: Goodbye. (*He stands up.*)

The two men go out. The professor sits down at his desk again and laughs.

PROFESSOR: Well, that was fun! Now we must wait and see.

Scene 3

It is about eleven o'clock. The professor is still looking at the papers on his desk. Miss Green runs into the room.

MISS GREEN: Oh professor! Those two men! Have they left?

PROFESSOR (*looking up*): Yes, of course they've left, Miss Green. They've taken the papers and they've gone back to London.

MISS GREEN: Oh, that's terrible!

PROFESSOR: What's terrible? What are you talking about? Explain yourself.

MISS GREEN (*beginning to cry*): They were the wrong men, professor!

PROFESSOR: I don't understand. You looked at their cards, didn't you?

MISS GREEN: I know. But they *stole* those cards.

PROFESSOR: How do you know?

MISS GREEN: The police telephoned. The right men were coming from London. These men stopped the car. They

Have they left?

shut the men in an empty house and stole all their papers. And now they've stolen your invention. What are we going to do?

At that moment the doorbell rings.

PROFESSOR: Go and open the door, Miss Green. It may be the police.

Miss Green goes out of the room. She comes back with two policemen.

INSPECTOR: I'm Inspector Hadley, sir. And this is Sergeant Bull.

It isn't necessary, inspector

PROFESSOR: Please take a seat.

The inspector and the sergeant sit down. The inspector puts his hat on the professor's desk.

INSPECTOR: So those men have taken your papers and already left. Your secretary has told us. But describe the men, professor, and we'll try to catch them.

PROFESSOR: It isn't necessary, inspector.

INSPECTOR: Not necessary? I don't understand, sir. These men have stolen your invention.

PROFESSOR: Oh, the papers aren't very important.

MISS GREEN: What are you saying, professor? You've worked hard. You wanted to give your invention to the country. Now these men will sell it and make money.

PROFESSOR: Yes, I worked hard. That's true. But those two men won't sell my invention.

INSPECTOR: Why not?

PROFESSOR: Because I didn't give it to them!

MISS GREEN: Oh!

PROFESSOR: I'll explain. When I saw the men, I didn't like them. You looked at their cards, Miss Green, but I had to be certain. I couldn't give my invention to the wrong men, could I?

INSPECTOR: So what did you do?

PROFESSOR: Well, Dr Fitt said he knew about my invention. He said they talked about it. But that wasn't possible. Only very important people knew about my invention.

MISS GREEN: You were quite right.

PROFESSOR: I gave Dr Fitt some old papers. He read them and he accepted them. So he didn't know about my invention. I knew he wasn't the right man.

INSPECTOR: So you've still got the papers?

PROFESSOR: Yes, they're on my desk. They were there all the time.

INSPECTOR: But we must try to catch those men, professor. Can you describe them to us?

PROFESSOR: Let me see. (*He thinks.*) Dr Fitt was short and fat. And he had no hair.

MISS GREEN: No, professor. That was Mr Rose. Dr Fitt was tall and thin.

PROFESSOR: Are you sure? Well, perhaps you're right. I can't remember things like that.

INSPECTOR (*standing up*): It doesn't matter, professor. We mustn't waste your time. Miss Green will describe the men for us.

The sergeant stands up too. Both men go to the door.

PROFESSOR: You've forgotten your hat, inspector! (*He gives the hat to the inspector.*) Oh, Miss Green. I'll go to London

You've forgotten your hat!

after all. I'll take the papers there myself. Telephone and say I'll come on Monday.

MISS GREEN: Very well, professor.

Miss Green and the two policemen go out. The professor sits down at his desk again.

PROFESSOR (*to himself*): Now for some work! Hm, where did I put my glasses?

THE END

STRESS AND INTONATION EXERCISES

Introductory Note

These exercises in the Structural Readers (Play Series) Stages 3–6 cover step by step some of the basic features of stress and intonation in English. If they are done carefully and practised regularly, they will help to improve the students' reading aloud.

In a typical English sentence, only words that are important for the meaning are stressed: that is, they are said more loudly and therefore heard more clearly. These words, for the most part, are nouns, main verbs, adjectives and adverbs. Here are some examples with the stressed words or syllables marked like this: '

1 She 'gave him a 'book for his 'birthday.
2 'John has 'borrowed some 'money.
3 I 'didn't 'know that she had re'fused to 'do it.

There is one very important thing to notice: stressed syllables are said with a fairly regular beat, and the lightly stressed syllables that come between them are hurried over to maintain that beat. For example, each of these sentences takes about the same length of time to say, because they all have the same number of stressed syllables.

1 'John 'drinks 'milk.
2 'Tom has 'cut his 'hand.
3 'Fred has been 'cutting the 'grass.
4 'Mary has been 'looking at my 'book.

Intonation is the tune with which an utterance is said. In general, the voice falls or rises on the last important stressed syllable in the sentence. Stressed syllables before the fall or rise are said on a level note, starting high and descending stepwise. Here are some examples.

1 TUNE 1 (FALL)
   'Mary 'gave her 'brother a `book.

2 TUNE 2 (RISE)

'Did she 'give him a 'new pen?

If there are any unstressed syllables before the first stressed syllable, these are said on a low note. Unstressed syllables after the fall are also said on a low note.

3 I'm 'going to 'give you a 'book for your ˋbirthday.

If there are any unstressed syllables after the rise, the voice continues to go up on these.

4 'Will you 'come to ˎtown with me?

Statements, commands and questions beginning with a word like *What . . . ? When . . . ?* are generally said with a falling intonation. Requests and questions beginning with an auxiliary verb like *Did . . . ? Can . . . ?* are usually said with a rising intonation.

Procedure The teacher should first read the practice sentences aloud to the class. Then the students, either individually or in groups, should repeat each sentence after the teacher. If the initial practice is in chorus, this should be followed up with some individual practice.

Exercise 1 Each of these sentences contains three syllables. At the head of each group the stress pattern is shown : stressed syllables are indicated by a big X and lightly stressed syllables by a small x. Repeat each sentence three times after your teacher.

(a) *Stress Pattern :* X x X

'bring a ˋfriend / 'sing a ˋsong / 'go to ˋsleep / 'wash your ˋhands / 'take them ˋoff / 'come aˋgain / 'don't reˋply / 'don't forˋget / 'father's ˋlate / 'mother's ˋleft.

(b) *Stress Pattern :* x X X

he 'sells ˋbooks / she 'swims ˋwell / they 'walked ˋhome /

69

we 'worked `hard / I 'don't `know / she 'can't `come / you
'aren't `right / they 'weren't `there / the 'clock's `stopped /
she 'won't `help.

(c) *Stress Pattern :* X X x

'run `quickly / 'speak `slowly / 'give `Tom one / 'don't
`drop it / 'don't `eat them / 'don't `listen / 'John `took
some / 'George `likes them / 'Joan's `bought one / 'Tom's
`seen it.

(d) *Stress Pattern :* x X x

she `likes him / he `told her / we `stopped them / they
`watched me / I `know them / it's `cleaner / he's `waiting /
I'm `ready / we'll `help you / they're `happy.

(e) *Stress Pattern :* x x X

she's my `friend / he's a`lone / it's cor`rect / I'm a`fraid /
we were `wrong / they have `gone / it's e`nough / she'll
for`get / they've re`turned / he was `there.

(f) *Stress Pattern :* X x x

`carry it / `follow him / `promise me / `read to them /
`speak to her / `look at it / `wait for us / `send her one /
`take them some / `make me one.

(g) *Mixed Patterns*

'wash your `hands / he `told her / 'don't `drop them / she
'can't `come / 'come a`gain / we were `wrong / he's
`waiting / `look at it / the 'clock's `stopped / `send her one /
I 'can't `wait / 'change your `shirt / de`scribe it / 'don't
`buy one / she's `pretty / they 'won't `pay / she was `glad /
'pick it `up / `stand on it / they were `poor.

*Exercise 2 Each of these sentences contains four syllables. Repeat
each sentence three times after your teacher.*

(a) *Stress Pattern :* x X x X

they 'weren't cor`rect / I'm 'not a`fraid / we 'won't
for`get / your 'brother's `gone / we'll 'come a`gain / he
'lost his `hat / I 'sent it `back / it's 'not e`nough / he 'left
to`day / per'haps she `knows.

(b) *Stress Pattern :* X x x X

'give her a `book / 'show me your `house / 'open the `door /
'bring him some `food / 'do it to`night / 'what does he
`want? / 'where did they `go? / 'when will you `leave? /
'what can they `see? / 'where does she `live?

(c) *Stress Pattern :* x X X x

you 'can't `stop him / he 'won't `help me / I 'don't `like
her / you 'aren't `happy / the 'dog's `hungry / he'll 'come
`later / your 'hair's `dirty / the 'train's `leaving / we
'weren't `talking / they 'aren't `laughing.

(d) *Stress Pattern :* x X x x

he `laughed at her / she `spoke to me / we've `looked at it /
I've `paid for them / they `came with us / be `kind to
them / he `promised us / re`member me / they've `eaten
it / she's `beautiful.

(e) *Mixed Patterns*

'open the `door / we 'aren't `happy / he'll 'come a`gain /
'what does he `want? / I've `paid for them / I 'don't `like
her / your 'brother's `gone / she's `beautiful / 'where does
she `live? / he `promised me / he 'won't re`ply / I'm 'not
`ready / 'what did she `say? / I `ran to him / it 'isn't
`right / they 'won't `stop you / 'why did you `laugh? / we
`sent them some / the 'bus has `left / 'where did they `go?

*Exercise 3 Falling intonation. Repeat each sentence three
times after your teacher, letting your voice fall on the syllable
marked* `.

(a) *Statements*

he 'lost his `head / they 'want to `leave / I 'know the `way /
they 'walked `quickly / she 'tried to `stop him / I 'haven't
'seen his `car / he 'doesn't 'like your `brother / they were
'all 'working `hard / it was the 'biggest 'plate on the
`table / we 'didn't 'say a `word to them.

(b) *Question-word questions*

'what did you `buy? / 'where does she `live? / 'who did
you `see? / 'why did you `do it? / 'what was she `looking
at? / 'which is the 'highest `mountain? / 'where shall I
'send the `new one? / 'how much 'money did he `give
you? / 'which 'house does she `live in?

(c) *Commands*

'wash your `hands / 'shut the `door / 'clean the
`blackboard / 'say the ex'ample a`gain / 'don't for'get the
`letter / 'come and 'see me on `Monday / re'member to
'buy some `matches / 'finish the 'work to`morrow / 'ask

him to 'pick some `flowers / 'tell him it's 'not
im`portant.

(d) *Mixed statements, questions and commands*

(i) A. 'what do you 'want to `drink?
    B. I 'want some `milk.

(ii) A. 'Where did you 'get that `pen?
    B. I 'found it on the `floor.

(iii) A. 'How did you `come here?
    B. I 'came by `train.

(iv) A. 'Come and 'help me in the `garden.
    B. I'm `sorry. I'm 'rather `busy.

(v) A. 'Wait for `me. I'm 'almost `ready.
    B. 'Be `quick. The 'bus 'leaves in 'five `minutes.

*Exercise 4 Rising intonation. Repeat each sentence three times
after your teacher, letting your voice rise on the syllable
marked ,*

'did she ˌgo? / 'have they ˌleft? / 'will we ˌwin? / 'won't
they ˌhelp? / 'has the 'clock ˌstopped? / 'can I 'come
aˌgain? / 'do you 'know his ˌname? / 'did he 'catch the
'last, bus? / 'have you 'made the 'same misˈtake aˌgain? /
'can you 'tell me the 'quickest 'way to the ˌmarket?

*Exercise 5 Repeat each sentence three times after your teacher.
Say the question with a rising intonation and the response with
a falling intonation. Notice that there are two falls in the short
form answers : `Yes, I `did.*

(a) 'Do you ˌlike it?   `Yes.
(b) 'Did you 'get my ˌletter?   `No.
(c) 'Have they ˌfinished the work?   Of `course.
(d) 'Are you 'ready to ˌleave?   `Almost.
(e) 'Was his 'story ˌtrue?   I 'don't `know.
(f) 'Did you 'give her e'nough ˌmoney?   `Yes, I `did.
(g) 'Has he 'answered ˌall the questions?   `No, he `hasn't.
(h) 'Is it 'necessary to 'go to the ˌbank?   `Yes, it `is.
(i) 'Have you for'gotten to 'wash your ˌhands?

                                                  `No, I `haven't.
(j) 'Did she re'member to 'buy the ˌbread? `Yes, she `did.

*Exercise 6 Repeat these dialogues after your teacher. Then
learn them by heart and practise saying them without looking
at the text.*

(a) A. I've 'left my 'pen at `school. 'Can you 'lend me
       ‚yours?
    B. Of `course. But 'don't for'get to 'give it `back.
    A. 'When do you `need it?
    B. This `evening. I 'have to 'write some `letters.
(b) A. It's `raining again. We 'can't go `out.
    B. 'What shall we `do? 'Shall we 'listen to the‚ radio?
    A. 'That's a 'good i'dea! Oh, the 'radio 'isn't `working.
    B. It 'doesn't `matter. I 'want to 'finish this `book.
(c) A. 'Are you 'coming to ‚town with me?
    B. `Yes, I 'want to 'go to the `bank. 'When does the
       'bus `leave?
    A. In a 'quarter of an `hour. 'Are you ‚ready?
    B. `Almost. But 'first I 'want to 'change my `clothes.